What Has
Black Spots
and Chirps?

WRITTEN BY **Robert Kanner**

ILLUSTRATED BY **Russ Daff**

dingles & company New Jersey

FOR CHARLOTTE GRANT

First Printing

Published by dingles&company
P.O. Box 508
Sea Girt, New Jersey 08750

**LIBRARY OF CONGRESS
CATALOG CARD NUMBER**
2007903696

ISBN
978-1-59646-788-0

Printed in the United States
of America

The Uncover & Discover series is based on the original concept of Judy Mazzeo Zocchi.

ART DIRECTION & DESIGN
Rizco Design

EDITORIAL CONSULTANT
Andrea Curley

PROJECT MANAGER
Lisa Aldorasi

EDUCATIONAL CONSULTANTS
Melissa Oster and Margaret Bergin

CREATIVE DIRECTOR
Barbie Lambert

PRE-PRESS
Pixel Graphics

WEBSITE
www.dingles.com

E-MAIL
info@dingles.com

The Uncover & Discover series encourages children to inquire, investigate, and use their imagination in an interactive and entertaining manner. This series helps to sharpen their powers of observation, improve reading and writing skills, and apply knowledge across the curriculum.

Uncover each one and see you can when you're

clue one by
what mammal
discover
done!

My **eyes** have excellent vision and can see a wide view of the grasslands where I live.

WHERE IS THE **EYE?**

I am able to hear
the slightest sound with
my short, round **ears**.

LOOK FOR THE **EAR**.

Long, black, **teardrop-shaped lines** run down either side of my face.

FIND THE TEARDROP-SHAPED LINE.

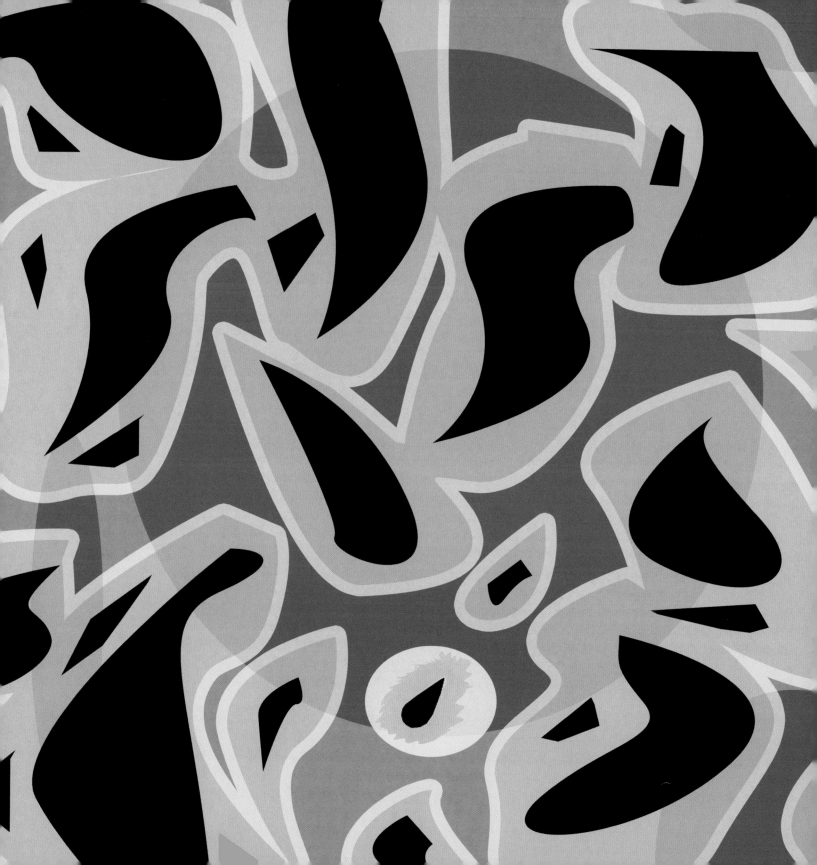

My **tongue** is as rough as sandpaper. I use it to groom myself.

DO YOU SEE THE **TONGUE?**

The **whiskers** on my face are very sensitive. They help me feel my way around in the dark.

WHERE ARE THE **WHISKERS?**

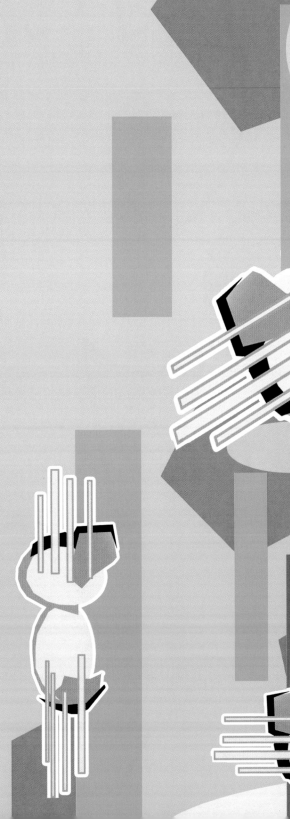

My large **nostrils** allow me to breathe in lots of air so I can run fast.

LOOK FOR THE **NOSTRILS**.

My long, slender, muscular **legs** help me run as fast as a speeding car over a short distance.

FIND THE **LEG**.

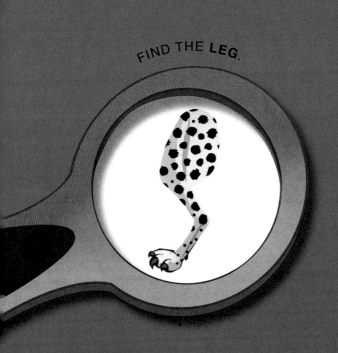

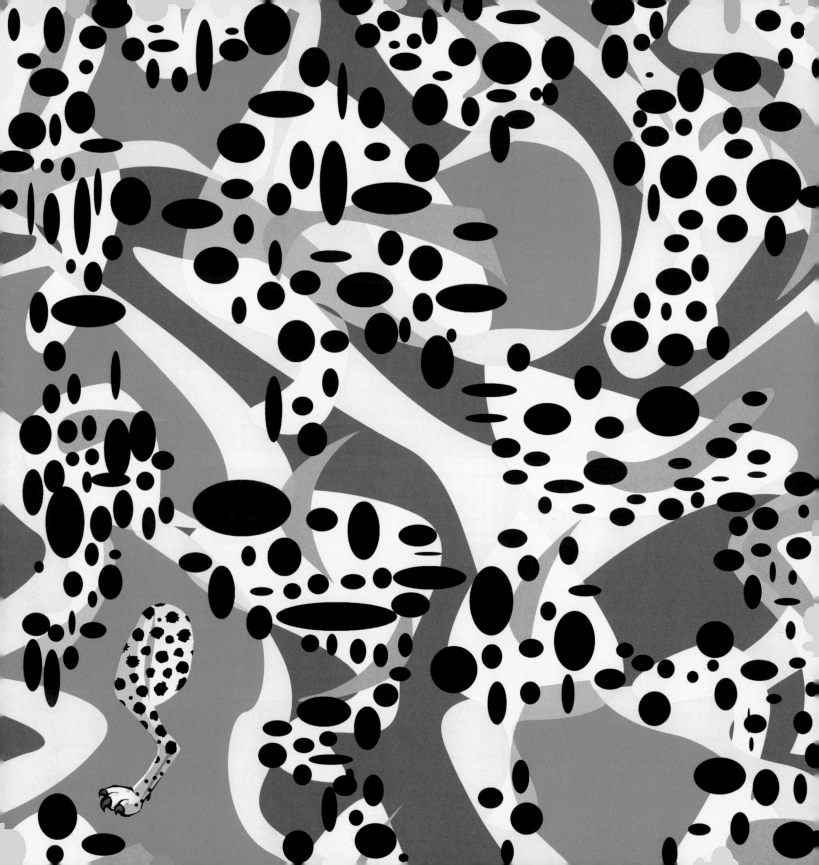

My **paw pads** have ridges that keep me from slipping when I run.

DO YOU SEE THE **PAW PAD**?

The blunt **claws** on my feet are curved a little bit. They help me grip the ground when I'm running fast.

WHERE ARE THE CLAWS?

A long, heavy **tail** keeps me from rolling over when I make fast turns while chasing prey.

LOOK FOR THE **TAIL**.

The **black spots** on my coat blend in with the trees and keep me hidden when I hunt.

FIND THE **BLACK SPOTS**.

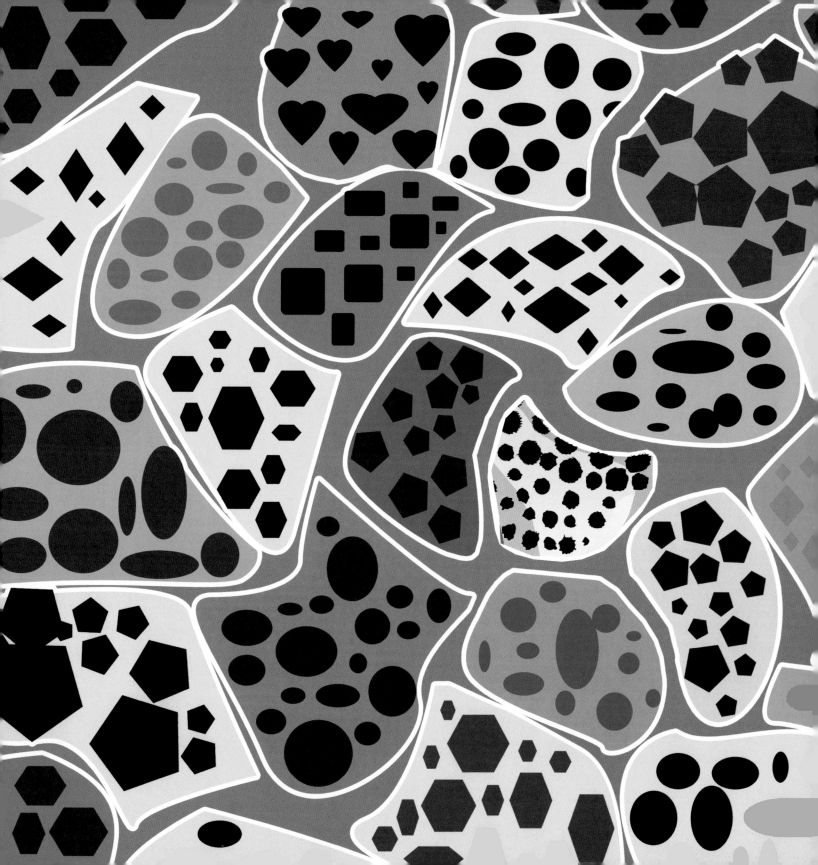

Sometimes I follow a **herd of antelope** because they are my favorite food.

DO YOU SEE THE **HERD OF ANTELOPE**?

9

You have uncovered the clues. **Have you guessed what I am?**

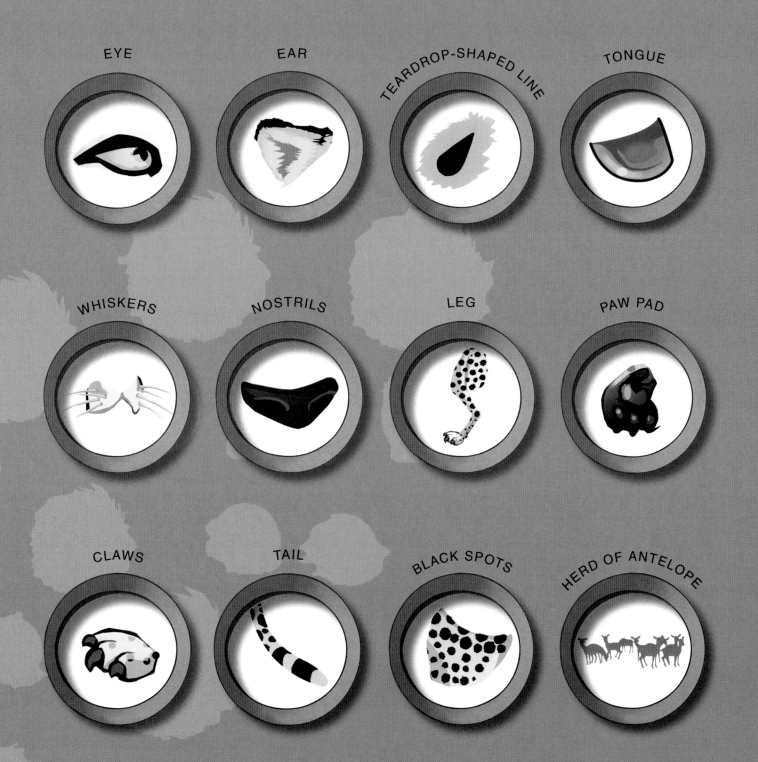

EYE

EAR

TEARDROP-SHAPED LINE

TONGUE

WHISKERS

NOSTRILS

LEG

PAW PAD

CLAWS

TAIL

BLACK SPOTS

HERD OF ANTELOPE

If not, here are more clues.

1. I am the fastest land animal on earth.

2. My average size is $1\frac{1}{2}$ feet tall and 6 to 7 feet long from the tip of my nose to the end of my tail.

3. I can weigh between 110 and 140 pounds.

4. I can live for 10 to 12 years in the wild and up to 17 years in captivity.

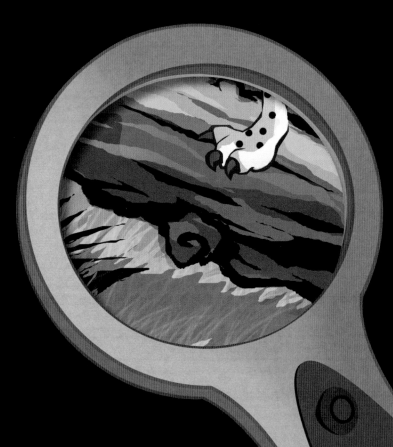

5. I mainly live on the open grasslands of West Africa and Southwest Asia.

6. I am a mammal. I have fur and was born live. My mother nursed me for the first 3 months of my life.

7. I stayed with my mother for a year before I was able to live on my own.

8. I am a carnivore, which means that I am a meat eater. I like to eat antelope, impalas, gazelles, rabbits, and birds.

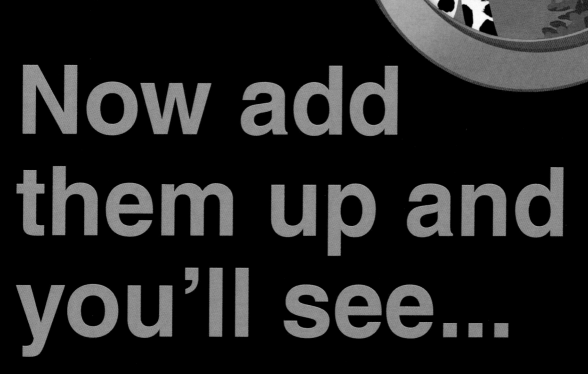

Now add them up and you'll see...

Do you want to know more about me? Here are some Cheetah fun facts.

1. Cheetahs are born in a litter, usually of 2 to 4 cubs.

2. A cheetah can run up to 70 miles per hour but only for 20 seconds. However, in that short period of time, a cheetah can cover 300 yards.

3. A cheetah can mimic the chirping calls of some birds. When a bird is tricked into appearing, it is eaten by the cheetah.

4. A cheetah hunts during the day.

5. Cheetahs usually live alone, although it is common for males from the same litter to live together. Females live alone except when they are raising their cubs.

6. Cheetahs are endangered in the wild because the places where they live are being taken over by humans.

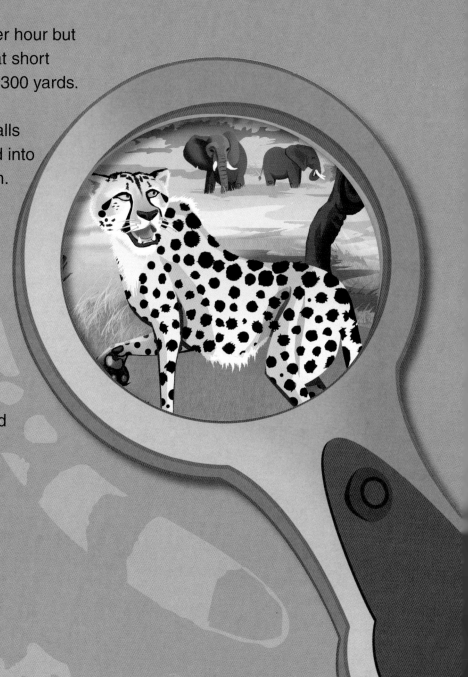

Who, What, Where, When, Why, and How

USE THE QUESTIONS who, what, where, when, why, and how to help the child apply knowledge and process the information in the book. Encourage him or her to investigate, inquire, and imagine.

In the Book...

DO YOU KNOW WHO is endangering cheetahs?

DO YOU KNOW WHAT the featured mammal in the book is?

DO YOU KNOW WHERE cheetahs live?

DO YOU KNOW WHEN cheetahs hunt?

DO YOU KNOW WHY cheetahs have rough tongues?

DO YOU KNOW HOW much cheetahs weigh?

In Your Life...

Cheetahs are the fastest land animals. What games or sports do you play that require you to run fast?

CROSS-CURRICULAR EXTENSIONS

Math

A cheetah spots a herd of antelope. There are 22 male antelope and 14 female antelope in the herd. How many more males are there than females?

Science

Cheetahs belong to the cat family. What are some similarities and differences between cheetahs and domesticated cats?

Social Studies

Using what you have learned about cheetahs, draw a picture of a cheetah in his or her natural habitat. Label the different types of objects and plants that are found in the cheetah's habitat, as well as the other animals that live there.

You have uncovered the clues and discovered the cheetah. Now imagine that you have a cheetah as a pet.

ASSIGNMENT

In ancient times, wealthy people kept cheetahs as pets. They trained cheetahs to hunt for them. Write a story about your pet cheetah.

INCLUDE IN YOUR STORY

Who did you get your cheetah from?
What does your cheetah eat?
Where do you keep your cheetah?
When did you get your cheetah?
Why do you have to be careful about where you keep your cheetah?
How hard was it to train your cheetah?

WRITE

Enjoy the writing process while you take what you have imagined and create your story.

Author

Robert Kanner is part of the writing team for the Uncover
& Discover series as well as the Global Adventures and
Holiday Happenings series. An extensive career in the film
and television business includes work as a film acquisition
executive at the Walt Disney Company, a story editor for
a children's television series, and an independent family-
film producer. He holds a bachelor's degree in psychology
from the University of Buffalo and lives in the Hollywood
Hills, California, with Tom and Miss Murphy May.

Illustrator

Since graduating from Falmouth School of Art in 1993,
Russ Daff has enjoyed a varied career. For eight years
he worked on numerous projects in the computer games
industry, producing titles for Sony PlayStation and PC
formats. While designing a wide range of characters
and environments for these games, he developed a
strong sense of visual impact that he later utilized in his
illustration and comic work. Russ now concentrates on
his illustration and cartooning full-time. When he is not
working, he enjoys painting, writing cartoon stories, and
playing bass guitar. He lives in Cambridge, England.